GETTING
unstuck

10 SIMPLE SECRETS TO EMBRACING
CHANGE AND CELEBRATING YOUR LIFE

GEORGE & SEDENA CAPPANNELLI

simple truths®
Your Destination For Inspiration

an imprint of Sourcebooks, Inc.

Editing by: Alice Patenaude

Photo Credits
Cover: front, Bertrand Demee/Getty Images; back, pridumala/Thinkstock
Internals: page 1, Yauheni Attsetski/Thinkstock, pridumala/Thinkstock; page 3, Amornism/Thinkstock; page 4, Roman Malyshev/Thinkstock; page 5, gepard001/Thinkstock; page 7, Ingram Publishing/Thinkstock; page 8, kameshkova/Thinkstock; page 9, mysondanube/Thinkstock; page 11, Kollibri/Shutterstock; page 16, Kiril Stanchev/Shutterstock; page 17, Kollibri/Shutterstock; page 19, Kiril Stanchev/Shutterstock, Akhilesh/Thinkstock; page 24, Kiril Stanchev/Shutterstock; page 27, Kollibri/Shutterstock; pages 30–31, Tinica/Thinkstock; page 39, Kiril Stanchev/Shutterstock; pages 50–51, A-Digit/iStock; page 54, Liliya Kulianionak/Shutterstock; page 61, Maksim Gorbunov/Shutterstock; page 66, Kiril Stanchev/Shutterstock; page 67, Kollibri/Shutterstock; page 75, Kollibri/Shutterstock; page 83, Kollibri/Shutterstock; pages 86–87, Tinica/Thinkstock; page 95, Boyan Dimitrov/Shutterstock; page 101, Kollibri/Shutterstock; pages 104–105, Oksanika/Shutterstock; page 107, author photo by Lisa Law.

Published by Simple Truths, an imprint of Sourcebooks, Inc.
P.O. Box 4410, Naperville, Illinois 60567-4410
(630) 961-3900
Fax: (630) 961-2168
www.sourcebooks.com

Printed and bound in China.
OGP 10 9 8 7 6 5 4 3 2 1

I DREAMT OF GREATNESS ONCE

by George Cappannelli

I did not start out to play
a small game or to do ordinary things.
I dreamt of greatness once,
of lifting my wings and soaring
to great heights.
Of charging the barricades
and fighting the good fight.
Of making a difference
and celebrating my life.

But the world around me,
the body that was my home,
and the skills
and talents I came into
life with were not perfect.
They did not seem to validate
my inner dream
of greatness.

So I turned elsewhere,
toward the practical things I was told
I was supposed to do.
I turned outward and away from
the promptings of my inner voice.
And I listened instead
to those who told me
my dreams were foolish,
that I was just like them.

And yet sitting here now,
looking back on the road
I have traveled,
I find myself wondering,
"Is this really all there is?"
And sometimes in the spaces between
the moments of my life,
I think I hear
echoes of my early dreams.

So I ask myself,
"Is it too late?
Can I still change?"
And from someplace deep within,
a soft yet persistent voice says,
"It's never too late or too soon
to follow your heart,
to get out of the ruts
of old habits and ordinary ways!

"It's never too late or too soon
to do the things
you've come here to do!"
And in these moments,
something stirs inside me.
It feels like hope and maybe passion,
imagination and inspiration.
And I know that this time
there will be no turning away.

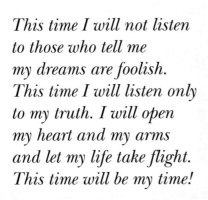

This time I will not listen
to those who tell me
my dreams are foolish.
This time I will listen only
to my truth. I will open
my heart and my arms
and let my life take flight.
This time will be my time!

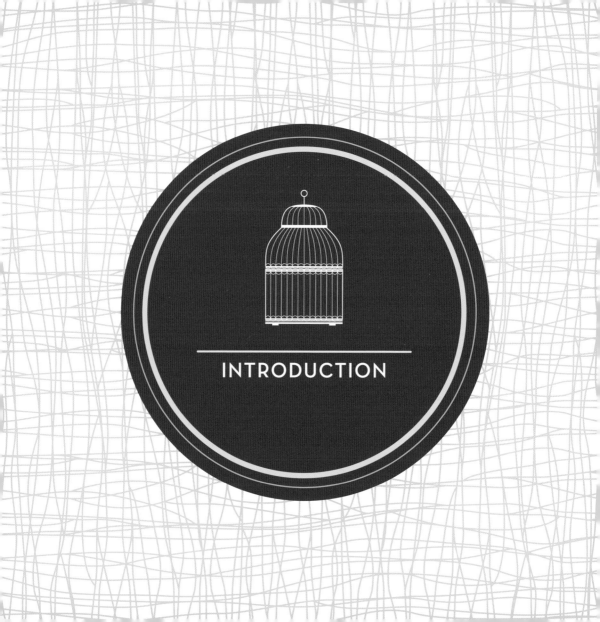

INTRODUCTION

Are you stuck in the rut of ordinary life, and do you long for the life you were born to live? Do you want to fully uncover your true identity and realize your dreams?

In *Getting Unstuck*, we will share ten simple secrets to help you embrace change and celebrate your life. And frankly, there's never been a better time to develop your skills in managing change. The world is changing at an astounding rate and ushering in a time of significant challenges, but also of unlimited choices and remarkable opportunities. As a result, many of us find ourselves in major transitions—making multiple changes in careers, geographies, and even our life partners.

Change, either positive, like births and breakthroughs, or what we think of as negative, like death and taxes, is one of life's true constants. But, positive or negative, changes sometimes astound and bewilder us to the point that we risk losing our balance. This is especially true when juggling life's external demands with ones that come from our hearts. It can make us feel that we are on a tightrope high above the ground without a net. At such times, we risk losing not only our footing, but also our enthusiasm, energy, and passion for the dreams we want to accomplish.

So remember that even when we face truly significant challenges, life is always full of new chances and fresh starts. There is wonder and magic, hope and inspiration to be found whenever we open our hearts and minds.

The ten secrets you will find in these pages will help you keep your balance, stimulate your imagination, reconnect you to your intuition, awaken your creativity, and support you in making more empowered choices that improve both the quality and the experience of your life.

As you explore these ten secrets, we encourage you to be kind to yourself. Have patience with the process, take time to breathe more deeply and more often, and remember life is not a race. Indeed, if you are grateful for what you already have—both the opportunities and the challenges, the obstacles as well as the breakthroughs—you will dramatically improve your odds of truly living a life in which the best is always yet to be.

GEORGE AND SEDENA CAPPANNELLI

SECRET ONE

RULES ARE MADE FOR
THE GUIDANCE OF WISE
MEN AND WOMEN

"Logic will get you from A to B. Imagination will take you everywhere."

—ALBERT EINSTEIN

On the surface, life for people in different parts of the world seems to be different. And yet, when we compare inner needs rather than just external conditions or circumstances, we find that people everywhere are actually very much alike. As the poet Mark Nepo says in *The Book of Awakening,* *"What we reach for may be different, but what makes us reach is the same."*

Traditions and rules are also common to people everywhere. They are passed down from one generation to the next.

However, as valued as these traditions and rules may appear to be, they were not intended to be permanent. Instead, they are signs left by those who passed this way before us that mark a trail, help us to better reach a destination, avoid missteps, and master opportunities. That is the good news.

The not-so-good news is that traditions and rules can often become habituated. They cause us to forget that there could be different and better processes, alternate steps, and routes that can offer us new vistas and even better opportunities. These traditions and rules also can become so hard and fast that they are hard to get out of, like deep ruts in a trail.

While these old, worn paths may sometimes seem comfortable and familiar, they actually limit our choices and dampen our spontaneity, creativity, originality, and innovation. They become like the stakes we put in the ground to protect a new sapling. In the beginning, they give it strength and help it to endure the vagaries of winds and weather, but left too long, the ties can begin to bind, scar, and eventually cut off the very life they are meant to support.

RULES ARE ONLY TEMPORARY MARKERS

This is the advice of our First Secret:

The traditions and rules shared by those who have come before serve us best when we remember they are temporary markers to guide us. Like the sapling and its stakes, we would be wise to use traditions and rules only until we are strong enough to stand on our own.

When they limit us or cause us to get stuck, it is time to experiment with variations, make refinements, or develop entirely new traditions and rules more appropriate for our situations. This First Secret encourages us to use the rules and traditions passed down by our ancestors as stepping stones to build new strategies, discover new paths, and invent new processes. In this way, we honor and celebrate the contributions of those who preceded us, but do not allow them to limit our authenticity and the lives we were born to live.

Traditions and rules are like a base camp from which we can ascend to higher ground and more expansive vistas. They are starting points for our exploration of the new, the unknown, and the remarkable. They are not fixed positions in the valley from which we always must look longingly at the distant peaks. If we keep this secret in mind, then we too will forge new trails, add to the knowledge we have gained from our ancestors, and leave behind a legacy of trail markers for those who come after us.

GETTING UNSTUCK

Step One—Set aside a little time to get quiet and write down some of the primary traditions and rules that define your world. Ask yourself: Which of these traditions and rules may contribute to keeping you stuck, and which contribute to helping you live a more joyful, satisfying, and meaningful life?

Step Two—Consider ways in which you can refine or change the rule or tradition to better serve you and those you love.

SECRET TWO

BEGIN IN
THE BEGINNING

"The real voyage of discovery consists not in seeking new land-scapes but in having new eyes."

—MARCEL PROUST

As obvious and natural as it might seem, most of us rarely begin things in the beginning. In fact, given the opportunity, a lot of us jump in wherever we happen to find ourselves. Anxious for activity, sometimes to the point of compulsion, we want to get right to the task.

Many of us know that we should take time to identify our vision, articulate our goals, and create a plan of action that anticipates possible challenges and prepares us to capitalize on opportunities. We also know we would be wise to identify at least one or more alternative routes, establish a support group, seek out a mentor or coach, and take careful inventory of the resources and skills we have or will need. We know that seeking agreement on our goals with family, friends, and others who may be significantly affected by our choices is of great value.

And yet, most of us succumb to the illusion that time is running out, that we need to get to "it"—whatever "it" is—so that we can get "it" done! Worse yet, many of us try to get "it" done without even properly defining where "it" may lead us. In the language of navigation, we set off on our journey without first deciding on a destination, charting a course, or even understanding why we are taking the trip. In short, we violate Lucius Annaeus Seneca's sage advice regarding voyages:

When a man does not know what harbor he is
making for, no wind is the right wind.

If this tendency to jump into a task without doing some or all of these essential preliminary steps applies to you, then perhaps it is time to change your strategy. If you want to successfully navigate the turbulent currents of contemporary life with greater effectiveness and joy, if you want to get unstuck and experience what it is like to live in greater flow and harmony, then it's time to examine not only your task (the "what"), but also your process (the "how") and, most especially, "who" does the "how" that gets the "what" done.

Look not only outward, but also inward; identify ways to increase your skills; and remove any inner emotional resistance and fears so you will arrive at greater levels of self-knowledge and life mastery.

SOME PRIMARY RULES OF CHANGE

As you consider the "what," the "how," and the "who," you may also want to reflect on a few primary rules of change:

- » Change is unavoidable.

- » Change sometimes feels uncomfortable—at least at first.

- » Change is often messy.

- » Change takes time, patience, and commitment.

- » Change requires planning, perspective, and an investment of time and energy.

- » Change opens the door to valuable new possibilities, discoveries, and adventures.

THE VALUE OF VALUES

In order to make change your ally instead of your adversary, revisit and reevaluate your core values. Strong core values help us determine not only how we get to our destination, but also how much we enjoy the journey and how we will feel about it once we get there.

Core values are, in many ways, the building blocks we live by and for. They are the qualities and characteristics we admire most. Their presence and practice make our lives truer, richer, and more rewarding.

We do not require a long list of core values to lead a success-ful life. Four or five are generally more than enough: honesty, integrity, compassion, love, and courage may be included among yours, although the list is endless. These core values, accepted and practiced—not with obsession or attachment to perfection, not with rigidity, but with commitment and patience, humility and trust—can transform any straw in your life into real gold.

As you prepare for this adventure of making change your ally and gaining enough momentum to get out of the ruts you may be stuck in, reflect on and, if necessary, redefine or refine your core values. Use them as tools that will get you closer to your destination.

GETTING UNSTUCK

Step One—Take a few deep breaths and tune in to your heart. Then write out your ideal scene for the next period of your life. It could be a day, a week, a year, or a decade. Then let your heart speak as you write out your ideal scene. Describe where you are, who you are with, and what an ideal day looks, feels, and sounds like.

Step Two—Turn this ideal scene into a short mental video and play it over and over again in your mind. Experiment with turning up the sound, adjusting the color, and zooming in on details you particularly like. Feel the energy and excitement this ideal scene brings up inside you.

Step Three—As you play your video, if any old or limiting thoughts come up, any doubts or resistance, take a few long, slow breaths and replace these thoughts with feelings of gratitude. See yourself unencumbered and free of past limitations. Be especially grateful for the people in your life, the body that sustains you, the teachers and mentors you learn from, as well as the lessons and skills mastered. Be grateful for the earth that is your home, and be grateful for what lies ahead—the adventures, the challenges, the hopes, and especially the dreams that await your manifestation.

WILD GEESE

by Mary Oliver

You do not have to be good.
You do not have to walk on your knees
for a hundred miles through the desert, repenting.
You only have to let the soft animal of your body
love what it loves...

Whoever you are, no matter how lonely,
the world offers itself to your imagination,
calls to you like the wild geese, harsh and exciting—
over and over, announcing your place
in the family of things.

SECRET THREE

LEARN TO SAY *YES!*

"If you refuse to expect anything but the best, you very often get it."

—W. SOMERSET MAUGHAM

In a world where *no* is said with great frequency and often used to limit, deny, obstruct, and avoid, *yes* is an extraordinarily powerful and greatly underused tool. In *yes* there is freedom, energy, wonder, and surrender. Where resistance, tension, and stubbornness are often the by-products of *no*, *yes* can become our gateway to openness, greater joy, and a rewarding and adventurous life. This is why learning to say *yes* lies at the heart of this Third Secret.

If this is true, why is *no* so overused as a form of expression? Think about it. *No* begins for us almost at birth. In fact, it's been said that the average young child hears *no* more than nine hundred times for every *yes*.

For the most part, adults do what they can to make children safe, integrated, socialized human beings. They teach what they have been taught—that children need to be disciplined and given boundaries. But adults are also human, which means they are less than perfect. And the limits and rules they set are not always perfect either. Instead, like the ancestors discussed in the First Secret, adults pass on to children the beliefs and behaviors they were taught and have come to view as "truths." And they teach these "truths" by using the same method that has been used for generations—the word *no*.

Just two letters, and yet this word describes conditions of restriction and limitation. *No* is a powerful word. It is a full stop. It can feel harsh and deflating, especially for the enthusiastic child within all of us who seeks new experiences, spontaneity, joy, and a greater understanding of the world.

Unfortunately, after hearing this word a lot, many of us start saying *no* to ourselves and then eventually to others. Without necessarily meaning to, we express a lack of faith in our own ability to deal with the challenges and opportunities life presents. We also use it to express our distrust for others. *No* also distorts how we view and define reality, and when it does, it often contributes to our getting stuck.

This does not mean there are not times when saying *no* is a necessary and valuable thing to do. There are times of genuine danger, times when individuals try to convince us to do things that are harmful or seek to take advantage of or abuse us in some way. Under these circumstances, *no* is a valuable ally. But in truth, these circumstances are not the rule as much as they are the exception. Use *no* with discretion, lest it become our primary reaction to all that is new, different, and unique.

Test it yourself! Put down this book for a moment, close your eyes, and start saying *no* loudly over and over again. After saying it for thirty seconds or so, keep your eyes closed and feel what is happening inside you. Is your breath deep or shallow? How does your stomach feel? Are you enthused and excited or enervated and discouraged?

In the experience of many, saying *no* is constricting and confining. Breathing becomes shallow, and stomachs become tense. Many also feel anger and impatience. In fact, the majority of us find we do not like *no* very much at all. What about you?

THE REMARKABLE SOUND OF YES

Now, experiment with saying *yes!* Close your eyes, and for an equal amount of time, say *yes!* over and over again. Say it loud. Say it soft. Whisper it. Sing it out.

How does *yes* feel? Many say it produces an experience of openness and expansiveness. Where *no* is heavy and tight, *yes* is lighter, more joyful, and energizing. Where *no* is contractive, *yes* is expansive.

So here's your challenge—or, more importantly, your opportunity—to get unstuck and become someone who says *yes*. Today and every day for the rest of your life, proclaim your faith in yourself and your trust in the world around you. Declare your willingness to live more fully and participate without excuse, resistance, or holding back in the life you were born to live.

As you explore this opportunity, also remember that you can say *yes* in many ways to many things, not just to questions. Say *yes* to your dreams. Say *yes* to the opportunities that come up in your primary relationships, your career, and your friendships. Say *yes* to giving, laughing, and loving more fully every day. Say *yes* to the unexpected, to the unusual. And especially say *yes* to your beauty and your magnificence.

Even if the world around you is saying *no*, say *yes* to your life and to the original, unique, and undeniable you!

GETTING UNSTUCK

Step One—On a blank piece of paper or in your journal, make a list of at least five activities or experiences you normally say *no* to.

Step Two—Ask yourself if saying *no* to these activities or experiences prevents you from doing new things that could benefit you, expand your skills, or provide you with new opportunities.

Step Three—For each of the five activities or experiences on your list, do your best to identify a concern, discomfort, or fear that prevents you from doing them.

Step Four—Take a few moments and visualize yourself doing each of these five new activities and experiences, reaping a reward or benefit as you do them. Pay attention to how you feel.

Step Five—For the next few days, practice saying *yes* to as many positive things as you can. Start off with little things that uplift and encourage you, things that will make you feel a little better and stronger or that will produce a little more joy and enthusiasm in your life.

SECRET FOUR

BUILD A STRONG
AND STABLE BASE

"It doesn't pay to live in the past; there's no future in it!"

—TOM WILSON

Let's now turn our attention to other valuable things that can help us get unstuck in some areas of our lives and move ahead even more successfully in others. These additional tools can become terrific allies that will help us benefit from the winds of change and explore more of the remarkable opportunities life constantly presents.

No doubt some of these tools are already included in your ideal scene—a healthy body; a clear, active, and curious mind; positive, stable emotions; good financial awareness; and a deep personal connection to your core beliefs.

Identifying and then achieving these things, however, are two very different matters. So let's look at how we can create a stronger, more stable foundation for a richer, more rewarding life.

A VERY BASIC INGREDIENT

Let's begin with a basic critical ingredient—good old-fashioned honesty. You can start by using this ingredient to admit what most of us have always known but do not always remember—that no one is born with a perfect body, an ideal mind, and emotions that are always stable. Nor do most of us arrive on earth with a deep understanding of how the game of life is played and the role financial health plays in our ability to lead a successful life. However, these are things we can develop and learn. They can become allies that help us make the changes we want to make in our lives.

The next important ingredient comes in the form of a question: What are we willing to do to build and maintain a strong and stable foundation in each area of our lives? This is not always an easy question to answer, especially in a world where there are so many demands and distractions that pull us off course. If this is true for you and you really want to lead a healthier, more joyful and engaged life but have trouble answering this question with conviction, consider this provocative quote:

"If you think education is expensive, try ignorance."
—DEREK BOK

Or, for our purposes:

"If you think change is challenging, try staying stuck."

To arrive at whatever you define as a better state of physical, emotional, mental, financial, and spiritual well-being, you are also encouraged to bring patience, self-acceptance, persistence, and, of course, some good old-fashioned perspiration to the task. In fact, unless you get off the couch and start doing things differently and more positively, staying stuck could become a very familiar state.

MORE ESSENTIAL INGREDIENTS

When it comes to physical conditioning, you know what you need to do—establish and commit to an exercise program appropriate for your body type, age, and current conditioning; eat healthy foods in the right amounts; and learn to breathe more deeply to bring you back into the present moment where you can accomplish your goals.

Diet and exercise also play an important role in your mental well-being, as does your willingness to review and make adjustments to some of the beliefs you have accumulated over time. These beliefs may be sabotaging your mental well-being and undercutting your plans, hopes, and dreams.

Above all, remember that the most important ingredient you can invest is your personal commitment to do what needs to be done. Even the best toolbox is worthless if the carpenter does not open it and use what is inside.

To get unstuck and gain momentum, stay centered in your heart, and you will soon find support showing up in the forms of suggestions, people, and opportunities. All you have to do is have the willingness to listen and the courage to act on them.

Gratitude and blessings are two other essential ingredients. The more often you express your gratitude for every aspect of your life—for the fact that you are alive; for the people, things, and experiences that make your life possible; for the challenges and opportunities; even for the times and circumstances in which you get stuck—the more momentum you will gain to accomplish the things you want.

And blessing each and every aspect of your life—what you define as positive and what you consider negative—will provide you with greater clarity, courage, new skills and lessons, and a much deeper, more intimate connection to your faith.

GETTING UNSTUCK

Step One—Finding greater balance in mind, body, and emotions is essential to your success. Take a few moments and give yourself a balance score on a scale of one to ten in each of these areas: body, mind, emotions, and your spiritual connection. If your scores are relatively high in some areas, congratulate yourself for your good work and keep doing what you are doing. If some of your scores are not as high as you'd like, identify the area or areas where you can put more focus.

Step Two—On a blank sheet of paper or in your journal, identify at least one thing you can do in each of the areas where your score is not as high as you'd like it to be.

Step Three—Turn off the outside noise for a while, including other people's opinions. Take a few slow, deep breaths and turn inward. In the safety and privacy of your heart, allow yourself to admit that you really do not want to be stuck, that you really want to lead a more meaningful and satisfying life. Then, in humility, ask for guidance and support in remembering that "the best is yet to be" and have the willingness and courage to implement the advice you receive.

UNTIL ONE IS COMMITTED

by William H. Murray

Until one is committed, there is hesitancy,
the chance to draw back, always ineffectiveness.
Concerning all acts of initiative (and creation),
there is one elementary truth the ignorance
of which kills countless ideas and splendid plans:
that the moment one definitely commits oneself,
the providence moves too.
All sorts of things occur to help one
that would otherwise never have occurred.

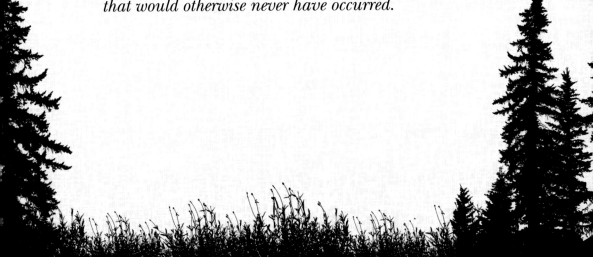

A whole stream of events issues from the decision,
raising in one's favor all manner of unforeseen incidents,
meetings and material assistance,
which no man could have dreamt would have come his way.
Whatever you can do, or dream you can do, begin it.
Boldness has genius, power, and magic in it.
Begin it now.

"You cannot put a big load in a small bag, nor can you, with a short rope, draw water from a deep well."

—CHINESE PROVERB

When it comes to identifying and changing some of the things that keep us stuck, particularly our old habits and limiting beliefs, all of us can be pretty stubborn and lazy, at least some of the time.

A lot of us also complain about life or wait for it to happen. Like the character in Samuel Beckett's play *Waiting for Godot,* we hope that if we pay little or no attention, whatever or whoever is prompting us to change might eventually go away. Or, better yet, someone might come along and do whatever has to be done for us.

Avoidance, resistance, and hoping for that free pass or the magical arrival of someone who will save us are things many of us are familiar with, especially when faced with significant challenges or major changes that force us out of the familiar and into the unknown.

If this is sometimes true for you, embrace Secret Five— Celebrate Excellence. This secret will help you discover a different way of experiencing challenges and uncovering new, more positive strategies to get your life out of those ruts and into real motion.

IT'S NOT ENTIRELY OUR FAULT

The truth is, our resistance to change isn't entirely our fault. When we were young, a lot of us were inducted into the safety and security club with the use of the word *no*. We were encouraged to turn away from what some called "our childish dreams" to buckle down and do practical, realistic things that would pay us a "living wage" and gain the approval and recognition of others. Drawing upon what they had learned, our parents encouraged us to do this not because they were mean or ill-intentioned, but rather because they had been taught to be afraid or uncomfortable in the face of the new, the different, and the unknown by their parents.

If you sometimes find yourself feeling stuck in one or more areas of your life, remember that it may, at least in part, be the result of things you've learned. Remember that by reconnecting with your early dreams and learning and doing new things with greater levels of excellence, you can stop being a prisoner of these limiting beliefs and habitual ways of dealing with the world.

Even in your most challenging times, there is a part of you that will always speak the truth if you are willing to ask and listen. This secret encourages you to ask your inner voice if it is possible to take charge of your life after years of being encouraged, trained, and rewarded for fitting in and staying between the lines. Then, based on what you hear, make the commitment to do so.

Remember also that not all of the challenges you face come from old habits or past programming. Some are simply an unavoidable part of the fabric of life. These everyday circumstances and challenges are things we all deal with; sometimes they make it hard just to get through the day.

Yet, as many of the world's great teachers have told us, although we do not always know why these cards are dealt to us, they are indeed our cards. When we reach down into the depths of our beings, we generally find the capabilities and resources we need to deal with the challenges we are given. As the old saying goes, *"God doesn't give us more than we can handle."*

TURN INWARD AND CELEBRATE

Remember to turn to that voice within you that speaks the truth. If you ask and are willing to follow its guidance, you will receive the wisdom and strength to deal with your life challenges and live the life you were born to live.

This Fifth Secret is a perfect complement to the practice of listening to the wisdom within. When you do everything—from the most mundane and ordinary task to the most challenging and sublime—with greater excellence, you can't miss!

This is a vital secret to getting unstuck and to celebrating the challenges and changes that are so much a part of life. But remember that "excellence" is not to be confused with "perfection." Perfection suggests an ideal state or condition to strive toward. Excellence, by comparison, describes steps in a process. Excellence is alive, vital, and always evolving. Excellence leads us to what is achievable, accessible, and ultimately outstanding. As Aristotle said:

"We are what we repeatedly do.
Excellence, then, is not an act, but a habit."

Celebrating excellence gives us the courage to be all that we choose to be. It calls upon our sense of integrity to persevere beyond the previous boundaries, restrictions, and fears that sometimes prevent us from reaching our goals. We must be open to learning, practice patience, and have perseverance so we can master what is needed to achieve the desired end result. Excellence is not settling for less, not stopping too soon, not defending the incomplete, and not justifying the inadequate.

So if living a life of greater joy, self-respect, and appreciation is on your agenda, become a lover and full-time devotee of excellence. You'll never regret it. Just do each thing a little better and with more love, and you'll never look back.

GETTING UNSTUCK

Step One—On a blank sheet of paper or in your journal, list five or six areas in your life you know will benefit if you do things with greater excellence.

Step Two—Write down one or two specific ways in which you can do each of these things with greater excellence.

Step Three—Close your eyes and take a moment to feel what it will be like to be more accomplished, satisfied, and proud of the things you do.

SECRET SIX

ELIMINATE LIMITING
BELIEFS AND NEGATIVE
SELF-TALK

"The beginning of wisdom is a firm grip on the obvious."

—ANCIENT CHINESE SAYING

Your mind may be hurting you. As long as you hold limiting beliefs and practice negative self-talk, it will continue to impede your ability to get unstuck and live a quality life. At the rate of 1,200 words per minute and 50,000 separate thoughts per day, your mind may contribute to your inability to experience the rich, remarkable tapestry that is your life. Comfortable with the status quo, your mind brings up resistance and doubt, convincing you that change is your adversary rather than your ally.

You may have heard the expression *"Be careful what you wish for because you just might get it."* Consider just a few of the people, experiences, desires, and material possessions you've asked for and fantasized about thus far in your life. That's a whole lot of asking. You might also want to consider the Law of Manifestation:

"Thoughts persisted in produce states of consciousness,
and states of consciousness, which, persisted in,
produce physical realities."

The wisdom offered in the Sixth Secret is that we create our experience and what we call reality largely through our thinking and the words we use to describe our life, both in our own minds and to others. Thinking can be a powerful and potentially dangerous activity.

Most of us engage in repetitive thinking and negative self-talk as if they were casual, inconsequential practices. We allow our mind to become an undisciplined and sometimes tyrannical master rather than a valuable tool and servant.

WE HAVE TO CALL THE SHOTS

When we abdicate our responsibility to direct it, our mind has no alternative but to fill the void. After all, somebody's got to call the shots. If we are not up to focusing our spiritual, emotional, and intellectual capabilities, or if we are not able or willing to live in the present moment, then our mind does the best it can to keep the wheels on.

The mind, like the computer modeled on it, operates on the information we allow in. And because the mind is also like a digital recording device, this information is faithfully captured and played back in images and sounds called "memories." If these memories contain limited thoughts and negative self-talk, they stimulate negative feelings and call up associated negative images and sounds in a continuous loop.

So how can we break this cycle? We can regain conscious control through physical disciplines like yoga, Pilates, Tai Chi, Qigong, as well as through contemplative practices like prayer, reflection, and meditation. In this way, we strengthen our consciousness and retake our rightful place at the helm of our lives. We can also replace negative self-talk with affirmations or positive statements that celebrate who we are and what we want to accomplish. And remember, we are as unlimited as we think we are.

Secret Six also helps us interrupt the continuous rerunning of limiting beliefs and negative self-talk and start more constructive, expansive, and positive forms of self-expression and envisioning.

GETTING UNSTUCK

Step One—Observe your thoughts and words each day. For a while, do nothing to change them. Just observe them and let this observation be your teacher.

Step Two—Once you notice particular patterns, write down some of the negative thoughts and forms of self-talk that may keep you stuck and that may limit your ability to lead a more joyful and positive life.

Step Three—Begin substituting new and more positive thoughts. Try on a new belief, replace a limited thought with a more expansive one, and start using forms of positive self-talk that reinforce what you want to achieve rather than what you don't.

Step Four—Do this for a while and pay attention to the changes that start to show up in your life. When you find that you are changing in ways you like, give yourself a reward that helps anchor and reinforce this new behavior. If you find yourself with more energy, more optimism, and more joy, you'll know you are on the right track.

> *"Security is mostly a superstition. It does not exist in nature, nor do the children of men as a whole experience it. Avoiding danger is no safer in the long run than outright exposure. Life is either a daring adventure, or nothing."*
>
> —HELEN KELLER

69

SECRET SEVEN

CONNECT,
UNDERSTAND, AND
ACCEPT

"Imagine what it would be like to live in a world where you are more concerned about what you have to offer than what you have to hide."

—UNKNOWN

This is a very powerful quote. It asks us to imagine a world very different from the one many of us live in. The current state of the world is better described by the second part of this Seventh Secret, a part not included in the title. The full secret says "connect, understand, and accept…don't protect, defend, and resist."

Why is this secret so important? To get ourselves unstuck from things that prevent us from living the life we were born to live, to spread our wings and soar, we must also remember that our world is changing rapidly. Although there have always been dangers and threats, they have been heightened with the advent of the information age and its instant forms of digital communication.

This sense of danger and threat varies, of course, from person to person. Some of us have never felt safe in our homes or in our personal relationships. For others, the boundary of our neighborhood, town, or nation marks the limits in which we feel secure.

Our sense of safety is also impacted by the major life transitions we all experience: job security, financial challenges, illnesses, loss of a loved one, aging, etc. Other broader factors also impact us: the nomadic aspects of the American society, which often separates us from our family roots and the geographies of our birth; dramatic increases in longevity, which leave us unsure about whether we will have the resources to support those additional years; and the astounding rate of technological, medical, and scientific change.

In the face of this, it is no wonder that we find ourselves a little breathless, bewildered, and sometimes resistant to change. And yet, if we want to get unstuck, live lives of quality and dignity, accomplish our dreams, celebrate our talents, and pass on our gifts and wisdom to others, we would be wise to take this Seventh Secret to heart.

If we do, we will get in touch with our own wisdom, forge new pathways, model new behaviors, and demonstrate that one is never too old or too young to live his or her dreams.

NEW CHOICES, NEW SKILLS, NEW FRIENDS

Follow the good advice of this Seventh Secret and seek to understand, connect, and be receptive to what is going on in each moment rather than reacting to limiting beliefs and habituated thoughts. Open both your heart and your mind, and set aside old prejudices and fear-based beliefs. If you do, you can make new choices, learn new skills, explore new friendships, and deepen your relationship with yourself and others.

Adopting this secret allows you to change where you may be feeling stuck. Where there is a perceived threat, there can be a new sense of openness and curiosity, empathy and accord. Where there is distrust, there can be greater receptivity, balance, and the ability to stay in the present more often.

This new approach will give you a new sense of freedom, new levels of energy and passion, and a greater understanding of the role you and your beliefs play in determining the quality of your life. That, after all, is what the Serenity Prayer counsels us, isn't it?

"God, grant me the serenity
to accept the things I cannot change,
the courage to change the things I can,
and the wisdom to know the difference."

In the end, it all comes down to a matter of choice. Each of us can choose to be reactive and at the mercy of a world that appears threatening, or we can choose to be open to life and its remarkable possibilities. We can be defensive and protective, or we can live with a new spring in our step and spirit, eyes that truly see, ears that really hear, and a heart that can feel the wonder and celebrate the magnificent mystery that is life.

GETTING UNSTUCK

Step One—For the next few days, observe if what you do most often is defend, protect, or resist. Keep a running list of these circumstances.

Step Two—Describe how you feel when you defend, protect, or resist.

Step Three—Identify the circumstances in which you have the greatest tendency to defend, protect, and resist. Notice what you think is at stake in these moments. What do you feel you may lose if you do not defend, protect, or resist? Ask yourself if thinking this way is worth the sacrifice of your self-esteem, effectiveness, personal power, freedom, and joy.

Step Four—Experiment with saying *yes* instead of *no*. Connect with others and look for ways to understand what is happening in the present moment. Pay attention to how this makes you feel and the positive changes that show up in your life.

> *"Hold every moment sacred… Give each its true and due fulfillment."*
>
> —THOMAS MANN

Unoriginal, overplanned, and *predictable* are words that can sometimes be used to describe the way many of us live our lives today. Controlled, careful, habitual, and risk averse are other words. In fact, in this complex and uncertain age, a lot of us find ourselves playing to not lose rather than to win.

We tend to focus more on security than discovery, on caution instead of experimentation, on safety rather than risk. In short, we sometimes appear to be more concerned about maintaining our tentative grip on what we perceive as our share of the status quo rather than surrendering gladly to the remarkable mystery life has in store for us.

This is understandable, of course. We live in a strange period in history, one that challenges us with its complexity and sometimes dulls us with its difficulty. But, we cannot and should not let our lives be constrained and limited by these externals. If we are committed to our own well-being, we cannot let our doubts and concerns overshadow the dreams and promises we came here to fulfill.

IF YOU ARE READY TO INHERIT
MORE OF YOUR LIFE...

If you are tired of living a restricted life and are ready to inherit more of the life that is your right, your privilege, and your responsibility to live, then this Eighth Secret is for you.

Amid all of the noise and confusion in the world, there is a place you can always go to find genuine support, encouragement, peace, and solace. This place is within you, where the voice of wisdom speaks. This voice will offer you positive alternatives and real guidance to help you discover a different and richer way of life. If it has been a little while since you last listened closely to this voice, it may be a little hard to hear. But if you give it a chance, it will reward you with all of the wisdom, guidance, and inspiration you require.

So start worshipping spontaneity. Feel free to do the unplanned, silly, illogical, and unexpected things that are suggestions from your inner voice. By doing these things—some of which you've been avoiding and resisting—you will break out of the prison of the ordinary and start feeling the excitement of the new and the different, both of which are valuable gifts.

Locate this inner voice and surrender to it. At first, it may only share vague impulses or slight hints. But keep tuning in to it, as you would to a signal on your radio, until you find the channel with good reception. "Turn left here!" "Leave now!" "Call him!" "Tell her!" "Don't go." "Dance." "Sing." "Laugh." "Share what you know." "Take that class."

Sometimes, you will get just a hint, not a complete blueprint. At other times, you may get something a lot more specific. No matter what the task, set aside all your procrastination and just do it. In the doing, you will find another hint. Like in a treasure hunt, each clue will lead you to the next burst of energy and motivation.

Above all, be kind to yourself and have patience. It may be that one of the steps you are prompted to take will appear to lead you to a dead end. Don't panic! Trust and await the next clue, and then follow it. It may be that there are long pauses between suggestions. Just continue to trust. No matter what the pace, form, or appearance, surrender to the rhythm, to the flow, and to the magic. Follow your impulse to say *yes* to life and to get unstuck. Let spontaneity be your teacher. Worship it!

GETTING UNSTUCK

Step One—Find a quiet place where you won't be interrupted. Take a few long, slow, deep breaths, focus on your heart, and for at least ten minutes each day, open a true dialogue with yourself. Quiet your mind, ask a question, and then listen to the suggestions from your inner voice that encourages you to be more original and spontaneous.

Step Two—Write down some of the suggestions from your inner voice. Pay special attention to the ones you are inclined to dismiss because they are risky, unfamiliar, or uncomfortable. These generally are the ones where you'll find real gold.

Step Three—Go over the suggestions on your list. Acknowledge some of the feelings that emerge when you imagine yourself following these suggestions. Identify those suggestions that run contrary to your long-practiced and habitual behaviors.

Step Four—Select one of these suggestions and visualize yourself doing it. Once you've had this practice run, go out and do it!

LOVE AFTER LOVE

by Derek Walcott

The time will come
when, with elation,
you will greet yourself arriving
at your own door, in your own mirror
and each will smile at the other's welcome,
and say, sit here. Eat.
You will love again the stranger who was your self.
Give wine. Give bread. Give back your heart
to itself, to the stranger who has loved you
all your life, whom you ignored
for another, who knows you by heart.
Take down the love letters from the bookshelf,
the photographs, the desperate notes,
peel your own image from the mirror.
Sit. Feast on your life.

"A fool is happy when his cravings are satisfied. A warrior is happy without reason. That's what makes happiness the ultimate discipline."

—DAN MILLMAN

Many of us spend a significant amount of time resisting change or worrying about almost everything. When we are not worrying, we are often doing our best to avoid other unavoidable changes that are a part of life.

Why do we worry about such natural parts of life? As we've explored in Secret Six, without conscious direction and guidance, our minds tend to run a continuous loop of limiting beliefs, assumptions, and negative thoughts and self-talk.

In fact, for many of us, worrying and taking things too seriously have become full-time occupations. We can sometimes parlay one almost insignificant thought or worry into a multinational conglomerate made up of a series of operating divisions called Concern, Doubt, Anxiety, Distraction, Obsession, Meddling, Suffering, and Fear.

In our experience, seriousness also contributes greatly to such common human conditions as foul moods, excessive weight gain, loss of interest and reduced levels of passion, the inability to smile and to sleep, stubbornness, arguments, isolation, anxiety, stress, troubled relationships, and more.

TWO UNFOUNDED BELIEFS

Seriousness often comes from the false beliefs that we are the center of the universe and are its masters and mistresses. These unfounded beliefs often lead us to live lives that are a lot less satisfying and joyful than they can be. Why are so many of us serious so much of the time? The real truth is that seriousness is a habit.

Rather than look for some obscure cause, however, our time would be better spent doing something about this habit that limits both our joy and our success. We can begin by eliminating the belief that seriousness is synonymous with importance. If we remember the Law of Manifestation, we know that continuing this belief only perpetuates it.

The next time you find yourself starting to get serious, look around and find humor in the situation. Throw back your head and laugh at life. Laughter, after all, is not only a wonderfully enlightening experience; it is also a divine prerogative.

GETTING UNSTUCK

Step One—For the next few days, pay attention to the number of things you take seriously. Notice if you use this seriousness as a way of making yourself appear busy or important. You may also want to observe how serious and "important" other people try to be.

Step Two—Pay attention to whether you get serious when you are about to do things that are risky, challenging, or that other people think are important. Notice especially how this seriousness affects your breath, the state of ease in your body, and your ability to stay present and participate in what is going on. Use a blank page or your journal to make notes on your observations.

Step Three—Try to find something ironic, absurd, silly, or humorous about some of the things on your list. If you have trouble locating the ironic or humorous side of these experiences, you can work with a classic observation technique. Visualize the experience in your mind and then—as if you are a comedy writer—introduce something into the scene that will make it funny. For example, have the person you are taking seriously stumble or fall out of his or her chair. Play some funny music in the background in your mental replay or have a dog suddenly appear in the frame, walk over to the person, and pee on his or her shoe. In short, find a way to take the serious and turn it into something lighthearted and silly.

Step Four—Make a commitment to look at what is absurd, silly, or humorous in your own actions and those of others. Practice letting go of your belief that you are more important when you are serious. And, above all, play more, laugh louder, and enjoy this wild and wacky ride called life.

SECRET TEN

BECOME AN INSTRUMENT
OF GRACE AND
GRATITUDE

"Join the great company of those who make the barren places of life fruitful with kindness. Carry a vision of heaven in your hearts, and you shall make your name, your college, the world, correspond to that vision."

—HELEN KELLER

Each of the secrets we have explored thus far, if taken to heart and incorporated into your daily life, will help you to move beyond some of the places you may be stuck. They will also help you start saying *yes* more often and with greater enthusiasm to changes that are not only unavoidable, but also valuable parts of life.

It is now time to explore the Tenth Secret. This secret will help us sharpen and hone our consciousness to an even higher degree. It counsels us to become an instrument of grace and to immerse ourselves in living a wonderful and loving life in each present moment. It encourages us to take the energy, passion, and power we discover through our practice of the other secrets and invest them in becoming more competent, grateful, and graceful so that we will be able to more easily lift our wings, open our hearts, manifest our truest dreams, and contribute to the well-being of others.

This secret encourages us to work on the places that still require healing and heal them, to identify things that are incomplete and complete them, and to build bridges of understanding and reconnection with the people in our lives.

It also encourages us to remember that we are not doing this for someone else. We are doing this for ourselves, to celebrate and master the greatest challenge of all—living our lives as a gift each day. Yet, by doing this, we also serve others.

No matter how seemingly insignificant the moment, action, or interaction, give yourself fully to it. Express your unflinching love and gratitude for the gift of this life. With genuine care, generosity, compassion, and always a touch of humor, become the instrument of grace. Let this rule be your guide, and you will need no other.

There are a few other keys that will help you become an instrument of grace.

» TRUST AND SURRENDER

Remember that your part in the grand scheme of things is not to always try to create the music, but to become the best instrument through which the music of life can be played. Remember that the mystery at the foundation of life is one of interdependence and cooperation.

» EXPRESS CONTINUAL GRATITUDE

Your life is a gift, even with its most daunting challenges, difficult people and circumstances, and significant changes. Begin expressing more gratitude for all of these gifts that make you stronger, wiser, more compassionate, more understanding, and more loving. Once you start being grateful for the more difficult things, it will be easy to be grateful for everyone and everything else. So take time each day to reflect on all of the people, things, events, and experiences in your life, and remember the wisdom the mystic Meister Eckhart shared with us: *"If the only prayer you ever say in your entire life is thank you, it will be enough."*

Rather than continue to look to the opinions or beliefs of others, take time each day to turn off the outside noise and spend time in the silence. It is the one place where you will always find genuine support, love, and the kind of wisdom that will allow you to lead the life you were born to live.

GETTING UNSTUCK

Step One—Observe yourself in relationship to the world around you. Pay attention to how much of what you do is done with excellence, compassion, generosity, and love. On the other hand, pay attention to how much of what you do is done primarily to gain someone's praise and acknowledgment.

Step Two—Take a few moments and describe how what you do makes you feel. Are you proud of what you do? Are you energized by it? Is what you do undercutting your self-respect, self-confidence, and passion about who you are?

Step Three—Look at what does not meet your highest standards, and identify at least one thing you can do to bring more grace, a higher degree of excellence, and more love into your life.

Step Four—Make becoming an instrument of grace your ongoing practice, and you will never look back.

WHO AM I?

by George Cappannelli

"I am only a person,
one person.
Who am I to make a difference?"
I asked.
Life seemed to answer,
"No one."
"I am only a heart,
one heart.
Who am I to think my love is so special?"
I asked.
Life seemed to answer,
"No one."
So I put my head down,
closed my heart,
and went about the business
of doing ordinary things.
But, one day,
after many pains,

more than a few losses,
and a whole lot of stumbles,
an obstacle greater
than I had ever before encountered
presented itself and said,
"You are one person.
You are one heart.
You are one love.
You have this life.
And that
is more than enough,
for that is
a gift beyond measure!"

ABOUT THE
AUTHORS

Photo by Lisa Law

George and Sedena Cappannelli are authors, consultants, speakers, and cofounders of AgeNation, a digital media company and social enterprise, and the Age of Empowerment, a 501(c)(3) serving vulnerable sections of our aging population.

They are experts on individual, organizational, and societal change, with an outstanding track record serving hundreds of thousands of individuals and hundreds of the world's leading organizations in both the private and public sectors.

George and Sedena are hosts on two national radio talk shows, *AgeNation Radio Magazine* and *Conversations with the Wisdom Keepers*. George is also an Emmy Award–winning film and television producer and director, has been privileged to work with a number of world leaders, and is an award-winning sculptor. Sedena, a longtime member of the Screen Actors Guild, has appeared in numerous films, television programs, and theatrical productions. Her new Personal Energy Program (PEP) DVD and book set introduces a series of groundbreaking wellness and enlivened aging processes.

Together, George and Sedena are coauthors of four other books:

» *Do Not Go Quietly: A Guide to Living Consciously and Aging Wisely for People Who Weren't Born Yesterday*

» *Say Yes to Change: 25 Keys to Making Change Work for You*

» *Authenticity: Simple Strategies for Greater Meaning and Purpose at Work and at Home*

» *The Best Is Yet to Be: How to Age Wisely and Fall in Love with Your Life...Again!*

They are also cofounders of AgeNation, the company whose mission is *to provide information, inspiration, education, products and services, and opportunities for the community and engagement for people who weren't born yesterday.*

AgeNation represents a constituency that will soon be 150 million strong with many things still to learn, much to contribute, and the opportunity to make things right with themselves and others.

To learn more, visit www.AgeNation.com.

ABOUT SAY YES TO CHANGE

If you like *Getting Unstuck: 10 Simple Secrets to Embracing Change and Celebrating Your Life,* you'll also like *Say Yes to Change: 25 Keys to Making Change Work for You.*

In our rapidly changing world, every person, family, and organization faces significant challenges, risks, and remarkable opportunities. Indeed, it is no longer a question of *if* you will change, but *how.*

In *Say Yes to Change,* George and Sedena Cappannelli, two of the country's leading experts on societal, organizational, and individual change, show you how to make change your ally, experiencing it as a doorway to new learning, opportunities, and levels of success.

For more information, visit www.AgeNation.com/store or www.SayYestoChange.com

"Real answers for individuals and organizations in a challenging world."

—Radio-TV Interview Report

"George and Sedena Cappannelli remind us that our fear of change, like our fear of so many things, blocks our ability to express love."

—Gerald G. Jampolsky, MD, author of
Love Is Letting Go of Fear

"In the work George and Sedena have done with us, we have used the concepts discussed in Say Yes to Change *and found them to be very valuable."*

—Brewster H. Shaw Jr., former vice president and general manager of the Space Exploration division at Boeing